I0818552

UNBREAKABLE SPORTS RECORDS?
HOCKEY
RECORDS
THAT WILL BE TOUGH TO BEAT
Carla Mooney
Mitchell Lane
PUBLISHERS

Mitchell Lane
PUBLISHERS

mitchelllanepub.com

2001 SW 31st Avenue
Hallandale, FL 33009

First Edition, 2026.
Author: Carla Mooney
Designer: Ed Morgan
Editor: Tammy Gagne

Series: Unbreakable Sports Records?
Title: Hockey Records That Will Be Tough to Beat

Library bound ISBN: 979-8-89260-726-1
eBook ISBN: 979-8-89260-729-2

Photo credits: cover wikimedia; p. 7, 9, 13, 15, 17, 23, 25, 33, 35, 37, 38, 43, 45, 47, 51, 53, 55, 56 Alamy; p. 4-5 freepik.com; p. 19 wikimedia; p. 27, 28 Shutterstock

CONTENTS

INTRODUCTION

Five Goals, Five Ways

On December 31, 1988, Mario Lemieux laced up his hockey skates. Lemieux played center for the Pittsburgh Penguins in the National Hockey League (NHL). That night, Pittsburgh was playing the New Jersey Devils. The twenty-three-year-old Lemieux was already a superstar in the NHL. His skill, **agility**, and power on the ice dazzled fans.

Lemieux was a natural goal scorer. The previous season, 1987–1988, Lemieux scored 70 goals. He won the NHL scoring title. In December 1988, he was already well on his way to another scoring title. Lemieux would finish the season with 85 goals. Fans called him "Super Mario."

In the game against New Jersey, the Devils struck first. They scored a little more than three minutes into the game. Lemieux answered with a goal of his own less than a minute later. His first goal was an even-strength goal. This means that both teams had all five skaters on the ice. A few minutes later, a Pittsburgh player got a penalty, leaving the Penguins short-handed. Lemieux took advantage of a mistake by the Devils and scored a goal. Later in the first period, the Penguins had the numerical edge. Super Mario came through again, scoring a **power-play goal**.

Lemieux was not finished. In the second period, the officials awarded Lemieux a penalty shot. He skated in one-on-one against the goalie. Lemieux took the shot. The puck flashed past the goalie. Super Mario scored his fourth goal of the game.

Mario Lemieux was drafted first overall by the Pittsburgh Penguins in the 1984 National Hockey League's draft.

Late in the third period, the Penguins led 7-6. The Devils pulled their goalie in the final minutes. This allowed them to put an extra skater on the ice. But it also left their net empty. With seconds remaining, Lemieux got the puck. He shot it into the empty net, scoring his fifth goal of the game.

Mario Lemieux had a legendary performance. He scored 5 goals, more than he had ever scored in a single game. He also scored each of his goals in a different way. It was one of the greatest moments in NHL history. Yet Lemieux was still short of breaking one record. The record for most goals scored in a single game remained unbroken.

Lemieux played for the Pittsburgh Penguins from 1984 to 1997 and again from 2000 to 2006.

Most Goals IN ONE GAME

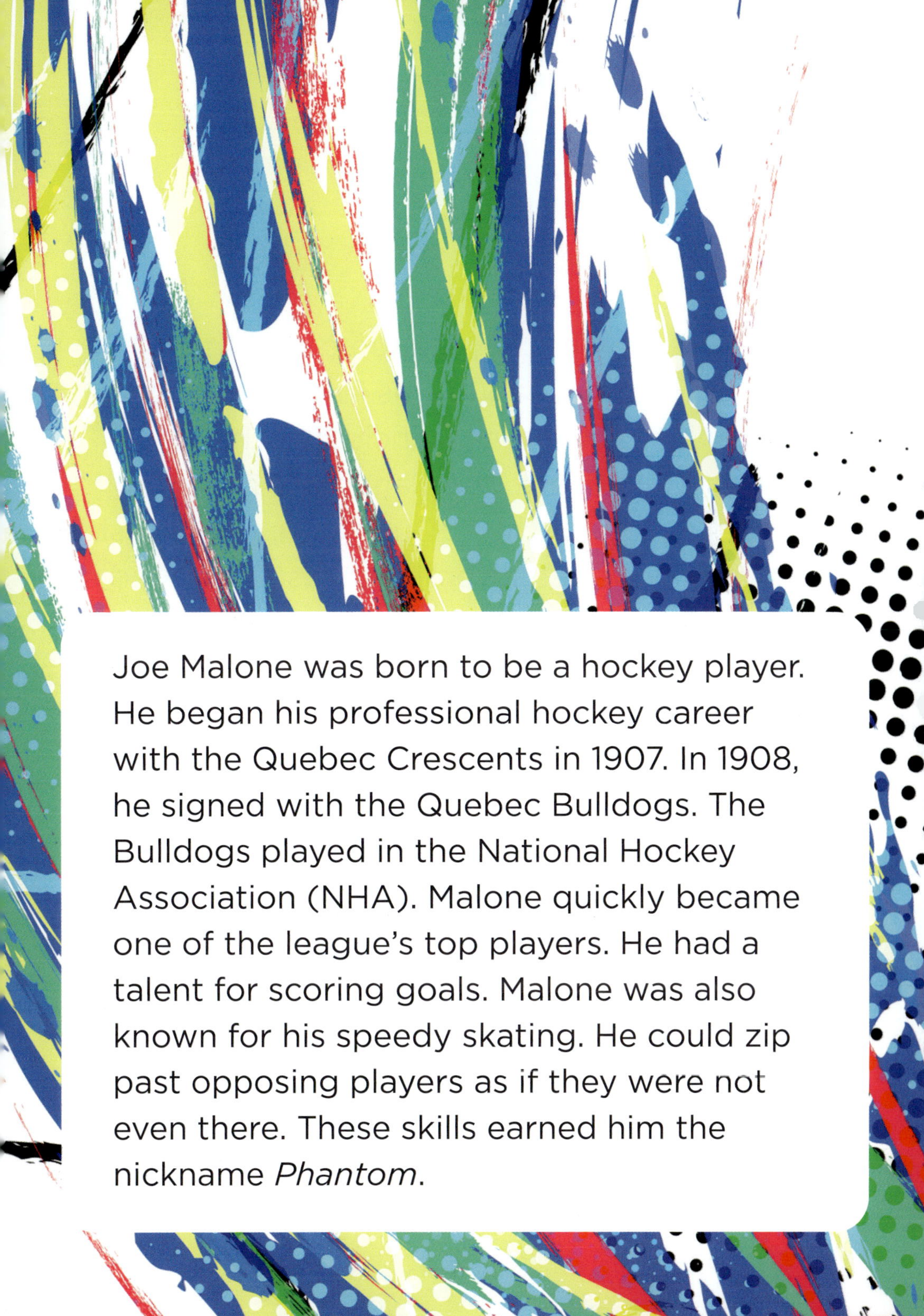

Joe Malone was born to be a hockey player. He began his professional hockey career with the Quebec Crescents in 1907. In 1908, he signed with the Quebec Bulldogs. The Bulldogs played in the National Hockey Association (NHA). Malone quickly became one of the league's top players. He had a talent for scoring goals. Malone was also known for his speedy skating. He could zip past opposing players as if they were not even there. These skills earned him the nickname *Phantom*.

In 1917, a new hockey league called the National Hockey League was formed. The NHL had four Canadian teams, including the Montreal Canadiens. The Canadiens picked Malone to play for them. During the NHL's first season, Malone set several records. He scored a record 44 goals in 20 games. Because of this accomplishment, Malone still holds the highest goals-per-game average for a single season in NHL history. Twice, Malone scored 5 goals in a game. Since then, no player has had more than one 5-goal game in a season. Malone talked about playing in the early NHL in a 1961 interview with *The Hockey News*. "I didn't have the hardest shot in the world, but I knew where it was going most of the time," he said.

MOST GOALS IN ONE GAME

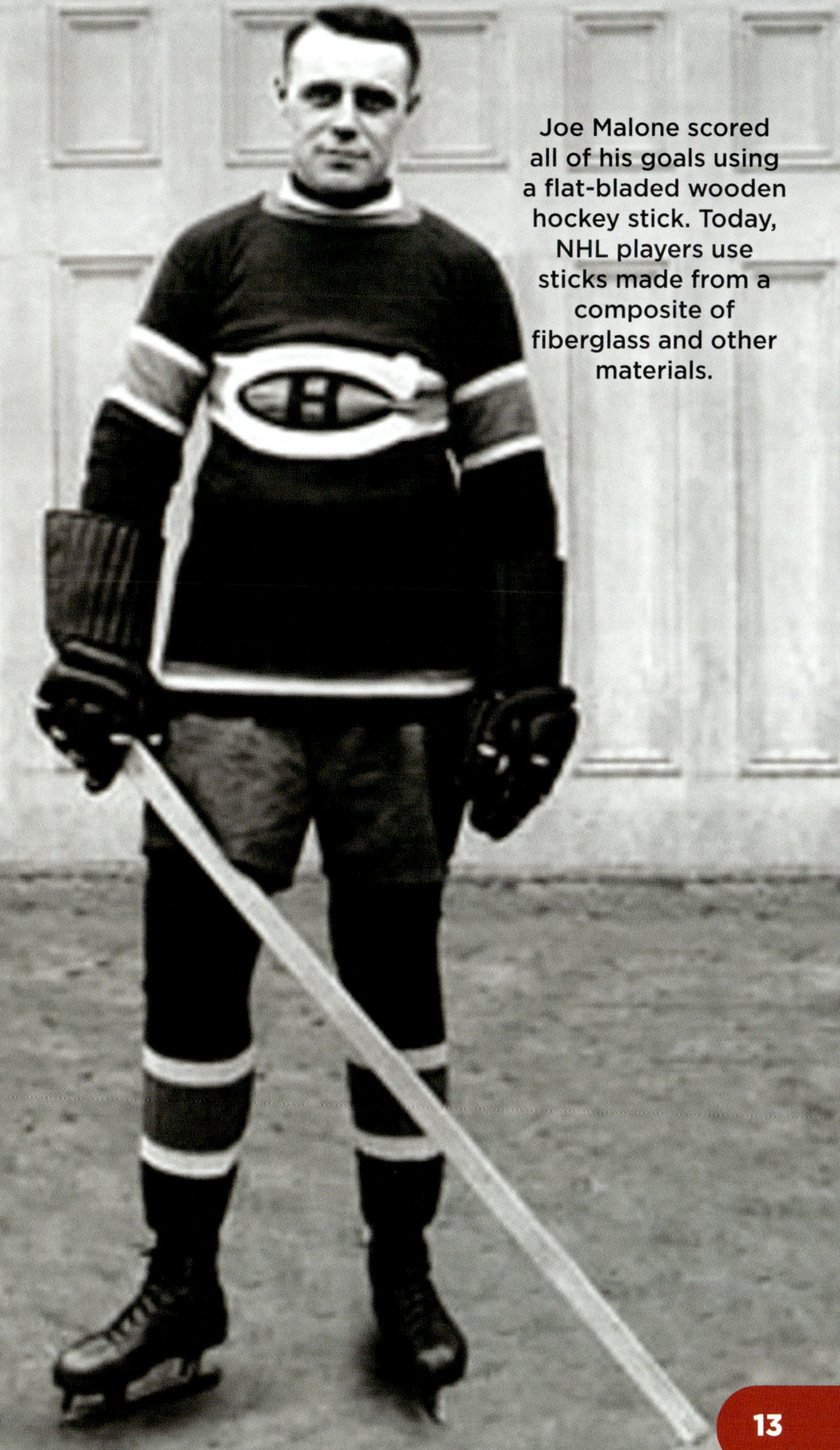

Joe Malone scored all of his goals using a flat-bladed wooden hockey stick. Today, NHL players use sticks made from a composite of fiberglass and other materials.

When the Quebec Bulldogs joined the NHL in 1919, Malone rejoined his former team. The season started slowly for the Bulldogs. By January 1920, the team had won just a single game. Malone's goal-scoring was one of the team's few highlights.

On January 31, 1920, the Bulldogs faced the Toronto St. Patricks. Malone scored the game's first goal seven minutes into the first period. Toronto scored quickly to tie the game. By the end of the first period, the Bulldogs led 3-2.

Malone scored near the start of the second period. A few minutes later, he scored again. Soon, he scored a third time. For the rest of the period, the two teams traded goals. By the end of the second period, the Bulldogs led 6-4. Malone had scored 4 goals.

Joe Malone wears the jersey of the Hamilton Tigers where he played for two seasons from 1920 to 1922.

In the third period, the score tightened to 7-6. The Bulldogs were leading, but the game was now close. Phantom Malone was not finished. He scored three more goals. The Bulldogs won the game 10-6. It was the team's second win of the season.

Malone scored an incredible 7 goals in the game. The *Toronto Star* reported on the game. The article said, "For the locals, Joe Malone was the bright star. The lanky forward had his biggest night of the year, setting up an individual performance that has not yet been equaled this year. He scored 7 [goals] and played a great game."

Edouard Cyrille

Whose Record Did Malone Beat?

Edouard Cyrille "Newsy" Lalonde was a professional hockey player from 1905 to 1927. He spent most of his career with the Montreal Canadiens. Lalonde was known for his slap shot and physical play. He helped the Canadiens win their first championship in 1916. On January 10, 1920, Lalonde scored a record 6 goals against the Toronto St. Patricks. He held the record for the most goals in a single game until Joe Malone broke it a few weeks later.

Malone played in the NHL until 1924. Over his career, he scored 143 goals in 126 games. Phantom Joe Malone was inducted into the Hockey Hall of Fame in 1950. Since Malone's record night, only three NHL players have scored 6 goals in a game. The last was Toronto Maple Leaf's Darryl Sittler in February 1976. Joe Malone's record for the most goals in a single game remains unbroken decades later.

Tage Thompson

Chasing Malone's Record

Joe Malone's record for the most goals in a single game has remained unbroken for more than a century. Since Malone scored his record 7 goals, only three players in NHL history have scored 6 goals in a game. None are active players. In December 2022, Tage Thompson, a Buffalo Sabres forward, scored 5 goals against the Columbus Blue Jackets. Thompson's 5 goals tied a Sabres record. But it was not enough to surpass Phantom Joe Malone.

CHAPTER TWO

Most Stanley Cup WINS

The NHL's championship trophy is the Stanley Cup. The iconic award is the oldest trophy in North American professional sports. It is also the only trophy in professional sports on which the winners' names are **inscribed**. Each year, player names from the winning team are added to a band on the Stanley Cup. Over the years, older bands of names have been retired so that new champions can be added. The retired bands are displayed at the Hockey Hall of Fame in Toronto, Canada.

CHAPTER TWO

Hockey players of all ages dream of winning the Stanley Cup. A select group of NHL players are lucky enough to hoist it as champions. An even smaller number have lifted the Stanley Cup more than once. But no one has lifted the Stanley Cup more than Henri Richard. Richard holds the record with eleven Stanley Cup wins.

Joseph Henri Richard was born in Canada in 1936. His older brother, Maurice "Rocket" Richard, became a star player for the Montreal Canadiens. Henri talked about following his brother in an article published on ESPN.com. "I wanted to play hockey because Maurice was playing hockey. But I never said it to anybody. When I was in school, they used to ask me what I wanted to do when I grew up. I never said, 'A hockey player.' I always said, 'A plumber,' or something like that," he said. Many people thought the younger Richard was too small for the NHL. Standing just 5 feet, 7 inches (1.7 m) tall and weighing 160 pounds (73 kg), Richard did not let his small size stop him.

Henri Richard became the second Richard to play for the Montreal Canadians after following his brother Maurice Richard to join the team.

CHAPTER TWO

Henri worked hard on his skating and stick-handling skills. He soon stood out in the junior hockey leagues. In 1955, the Montreal Canadiens invited Richard to their training camp. He made the team. Richard proved he could handle an NHL game's rough play in his first season. He quickly became a valuable part of the team that won the Stanley Cup for five straight seasons.

Richard's superior stickhandling and playmaking made him a star for Montreal. He earned the nickname *The Pocket Rocket*. Former Montreal general manager Frank Selke spoke about Richard's **impact** on the ice in an article published on NHL.com. "I have been blessed with a lot of great stars over the years. But game in, and game out, Henri Richard may have been the most valuable player I ever had," he said.

Whose Record Did Richard Beat?

Before Henri Richard, Red Kelly held the record for the most Stanley Cup wins. Kelly played as a defenseman in the NHL from 1947 to 1967. He started his NHL career with the Detroit Red Wings. With Detroit, Kelly won four Stanley Cups. In 1959, Kelly was traded to the Toronto Maple Leafs. On the Toronto team, Kelly played center. He won four more Stanley Cups with Toronto and retired on top in 1967 after his eighth championship. His record of eight Stanley Cups would last only a couple years until Richard surpassed him in 1969.

Richard and the Canadiens won the Stanley Cup again in 1965. In 1966, Richard scored the game-winning and championship-winning goal against the Detroit Red Wings. He raised the championship Stanley Cup four more times, in 1968, 1969, 1971, and 1973.

Richard played twenty seasons in the NHL from 1955 to 1975, all with the Montreal Canadiens. He won hockey's greatest trophy, the Stanley Cup, eleven times. For more than forty years, Richard's record has remained unbroken.

MOST STANLEY CUP WINS

The Stanley Cup trophy is awarded to the winner of the Stanley Cup Finals. The names of the players on the winning team are engraved on the cup's rings.

CHAPTER TWO

Sidney Crosby (left) and Evgeni Malkin

Chasing Richard's Record

As of 2024, Sidney Crosby and Evgeni Malkin of the Pittsburgh Penguins have won three Stanley Cups. Although a few other players have also won three Stanley Cups, no current NHL player has won more. Most hockey experts believe that Henri Richard's record of eleven will never be broken. Today's NHL teams must try to keep the best players despite salary caps and **free agency**. It is difficult for any modern team to repeat as Stanley Cup champions, let alone win enough for a player to break Richard's record.

CHAPTER THREE

Goals-per-Game RECORD

Every time Mike Bossy's skates touched the ice, he was a threat to score. Goalies across the NHL knew him as a dangerous **sniper**. Bossy had a way of melting into the background. A teammate would pass the puck. Suddenly, Bossy would appear as the puck hit his stick. His hands were quick. Within a split second, the puck was in the back of his opponent's net.

CHAPTER THREE

Bossy entered the NHL in 1977, playing for the New York Islanders. He had been a goal-scoring talent in junior hockey. Yet, the NHL scouts were unsure he could be effective against top defensive players. Islanders General Manager Bill Torrey asked the young player how many goals he would score in his first season. Bossy did not hesitate. He said, "50." No NHL **rookie** had ever scored that many goals in his first season. The record for a rookie was 44 goals. Torrey liked Bossy's confidence but doubted he could score 50.

In a way, Torrey was right. Bossy did not score 50 goals in his rookie season. He scored 53 instead. And he was not done. Bossy scored more than 50 goals per season for nine straight seasons. So far, no other NHL player has matched that 50-goal streak. In five seasons, Bossy scored 60 or more goals. He shares that record with hockey great Wayne Gretzky. Islander teammate Bryan Trottier described Bossy's mentality on the ice in an interview with NHL.com. "Scoring goals was what mattered to him most. He'd get mad at himself if he didn't produce in a game," he said.

MIKE BOSSY
ISLANDERS
RIGHT WING
NY
ISLANDERS

Bossy was an important part of the Islanders' championships. They won four straight Stanley Cups from 1980 to 1983. Bossy scored one of his most famous goals in Game 3 of the 1983 Stanley Cup Final. The Islanders faced the Vancouver Canucks. In front of the Vancouver net, Bossy was knocked off his feet. While he was still in the air, he pulled the puck toward him. Bossy shot the puck off the post and into the net.

In the 1980–1981 season, Bossy set out to break Maurice "Rocket" Richard's record of 50 goals in 50 games. No other NHL player had matched Richard's record in nearly forty years. Bossy intended to be the first. That season, he scored in bunches. Going into his 50th game, he had 48 goals. The crowd chanted his name as he scored his 49th goal of the season. Later in the game, he caught a pass from Bryan Trottier. Bossy fired his 50th goal in the last minutes of the game. He matched Richard's record.

Cy Denneny

Whose Record Did Bossy Break?

Cy Denneny was a **prolific** goal scorer in the NHL's early years. Denneny played as a forward for the Ottawa Senators from 1917 to 1928. For the Boston Bruins, he played a single season, from 1928 to 1929. Denneny was the fastest player in the NHL to score 200 goals, which he achieved in 181 games. In nearly a century, no NHL player has scored 200 goals faster. Denneny finished his career with a record-setting 0.75 goals-per-game average. Denneny held this record for decades until Mike Bossy broke it.

Bossy played ten seasons in the NHL. A **chronic** back injury forced him to retire in 1987. He played 752 games and scored 573 goals. He set a new record for highest goals-per-game average with 0.762. "Like Mario Lemieux, if Mike's career wasn't cut short, the numbers would be hard to fathom," said Trottier in an article for *The Athletic*. For nearly four decades, his record has remained unbroken.

Mike Bossy was selected fifteenth overall by the New York Islanders in the 1977 National Hockey League draft.

CHAPTER THREE

Auston Matthews

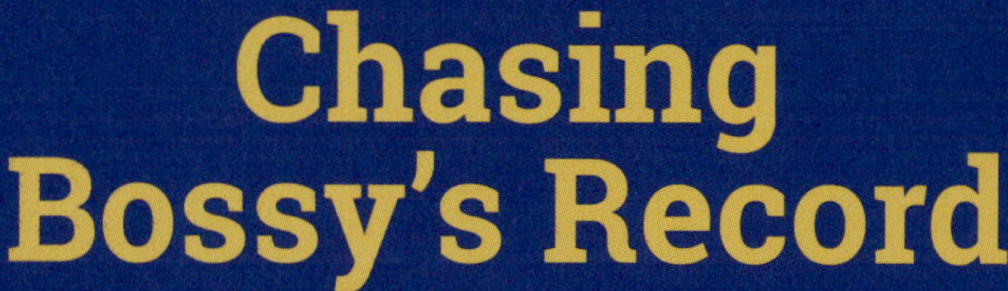

Chasing Bossy's Record

Center Auston Matthews was drafted by the Toronto Maple Leafs in 2016. The star American hockey player quickly made an impact on the ice. In more than eight seasons with the Maple Leafs, Matthews scored 373 goals as of November 2024. In two seasons, Matthews scored more than 60 goals, an accomplishment that only nine players in NHL history have achieved. By November 2024, Matthews' goals-per-game average was 0.65. That number ranks him fifth on the all-time list, trailing Mike Bossy's record.

CHAPTER FOUR

Most Career HAT TRICKS

Scoring three goals in a hockey game is called a hat trick. The hat trick has become one of hockey's most celebrated achievements. Many fans toss hats onto the ice when a player scores a hat trick.

It is not surprising that Wayne Gretzky, who is often called the greatest hockey player of all time, holds the record for the most career hat tricks, with 50. And that is just one of his records. Gretzky, known worldwide as "The Great One," currently holds sixty-one NHL records. He is the NHL all-time leader in goals, assists, points, and more.

CHAPTER FOUR

Gretzky first learned to skate at age two. His father took him skating near his hometown of Brantford, Ontario. The little boy took to the ice quickly, and his father built him a backyard rink. Young Gretzky could skate all day and night.

By age five, Gretzky played for an all-star hockey team. His teammates were several years older than him. Gretzky quickly moved up Canada's youth and junior hockey ranks. He scored goals everywhere he played. Hockey fans across North America took notice of the talented teen.

In 1979, Gretzky laced up his skates for his first NHL game. It was against the Edmonton Oilers. Gretzky dazzled hockey fans with his incredible talent. He scored more than 200 points, including goals and assists, in four seasons. He also destroyed the record of 50 goals in 50 games, shared by Maurice Richard and Mike Bossy. Gretzky reached 50 goals in just 39 games. He led the Oilers to four Stanley Cup championships between 1984 and 1988.

The New York Rangers signed Wayne Gretzky as a free agent in 1996. He played for the Rangers for three seasons before retiring in 1999.

Gretzky went on to play for the Los Angeles Kings, St. Louis Blues, and New York Rangers. He continued racking up goals and assists with each team. With the Kings, Gretzky passed Gordie Howe as the NHL's all-time regular season goal leader. Gretzky talked about breaking Howe's records in an article for *The Players' Tribune*. "Gordie Howe was such a great player, and to me, the greatest player that ever lived, and I always felt a little guilty that I was breaking his records, because it was such a different era when he played compared to when I played," he said.

Gretzky finished his amazing career with 894 regular season goals. This record still stands as of 2024. Gretzky also holds the record for most regular season and playoff career goals with 1,016. Gretsky scored his final hat trick on October 11, 1997. The game was a 6-3 win for his New York Rangers against the Vancouver Canucks. No other NHL player has even come close to Gretzky's hat-trick record. The second-place holder, Mario Lemieux, had 40 career hat tricks.

Phil Esposito

Whose Record Did Gretsky Beat?

Before Wayne Gretzky became a household name, Phil Esposito was scoring hat tricks for the Chicago Blackhawks, Boston Bruins, and New York Rangers. Esposito played from 1963 to 1981. He liked to play in front of his opponent's net. That is where he scored many of his goals. Over his eighteen NHL seasons, Esposito scored 717 regular season goals and 32 hat tricks. Although it was an impressive total, the record did not stand a chance against Gretzky's talent for putting the puck in the net.

Hockey legend Gordie Howe congratulated Gretzky for breaking his all-time career goals record. "You don't get called The Great One unless you're something special, and Wayne, it goes without saying, was a once-in-a-generation talent. Watching his artistry on the ice was a treat for everyone who loves the game of hockey," Howe wrote in his autobiography.

Alex Ovechkin

Chasing Gretsky's Record

Russian Alex Ovechkin is considered by many to be the best goal-scorer of the twenty-first century. Currently playing in his twentieth NHL season, Ovechkin has scored 863 regular season goals as of November 2024. He may surpass Wayne Gretzky's all-time goal record of 894. Ovechkin is known for his deadly slap shot from the top of the left circle and his speed and skill on the ice. While he may crack Gretzky's regular season goals record, Ovechkin's career hat trick total of 30 remains well behind Gretzky's record so far.

CHAPTER FIVE

Most Career SHUTOUTS

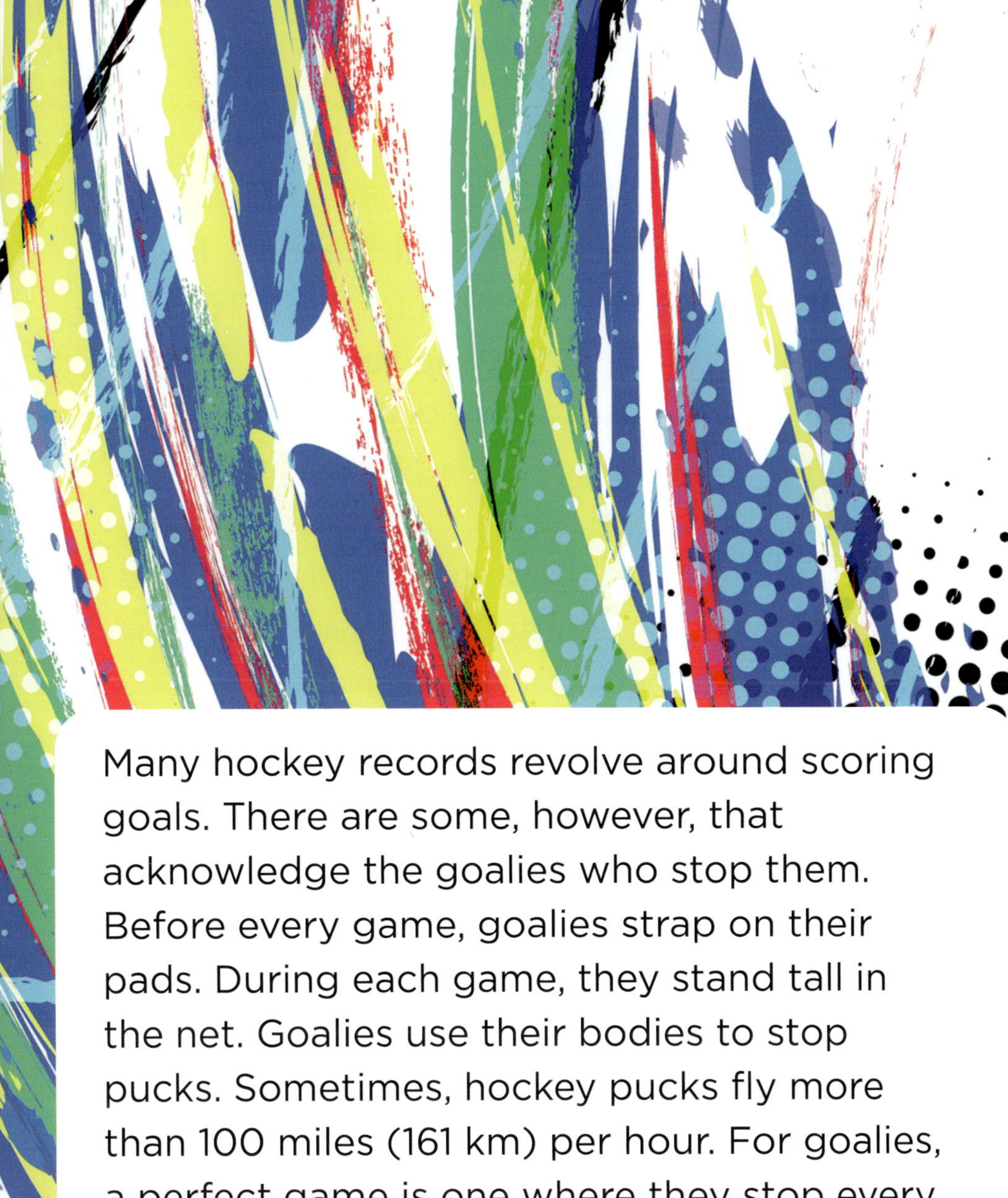

Many hockey records revolve around scoring goals. There are some, however, that acknowledge the goalies who stop them. Before every game, goalies strap on their pads. During each game, they stand tall in the net. Goalies use their bodies to stop pucks. Sometimes, hockey pucks fly more than 100 miles (161 km) per hour. For goalies, a perfect game is one where they stop every puck. An entire game in which a goalie holds an opponent scoreless is called a shutout. Hall of Fame goalie Martin Brodeur holds the record for most career shutouts at 125.

CHAPTER FIVE

Brodeur grew up in Montreal, Canada. He started his hockey career as a forward. He agreed to play back-up goalie for a second team at age six. The following year, he took over as the starting goalie. He always wanted to play for the entire game. "I learned the way you play will decide the outcome of the game and that was a fun pressure to have," Brodeur said in an interview with NHL.com.

He played his first season in the NHL from 1993 to 1994 as a member of the New Jersey Devils. Brodeur won the Calder Trophy. This award is given to the top NHL rookie. The following season, he helped the Devils win the Stanley Cup. Brodeur helped the Devils win two more Stanley Cup championships, in 2000 and 2003. He earned many honors in his career. He won four Vezina Trophies for the NHL's best goaltender. He won the Jennings Trophy five times for allowing the fewest goals.

Martin Brodeur reaches with his glove to stop the puck before it goes in the net.

Shooters often found Brodeur unpredictable in the net. "I could come down the right side three different times and shoot the same shot, and he'd make three different saves," Ottawa Senators forward Daniel Alfredsson said in an interview with NHL.com. Brodeur had a gift that allowed him to **anticipate** what a shooter would do. "I think he knew where the puck was going to be before any of the shooters did," said teammate and goalie Cory Schneider in an interview with NHL.com.

Brodeur sits atop the NHL record book for goalies. In addition to this record for the most shutouts, he has NHL records for the most wins, with 691, and most games, with 1,266. He was also the youngest goalie to reach 300 wins.

George Hainsworth

Whose Record Did Brodeur Beat?

George Hainsworth was a top goalie in Canada before the NHL began. He played professionally in the Western Canada Hockey League for three seasons before signing with the NHL's Montreal Canadiens in 1926. The Canadiens needed a goaltender after their goalie, George Vezina, passed away from **tuberculosis**. The team created the Vezina Trophy for the top NHL goalie in his honor in 1927. Hainsworth won the trophy for its first three seasons, from 1927 to 1929. He recorded 94 NHL shutouts during his career. He is now third on the all-time list behind Martin Brodeur and Terry Sawchuk.

Teammates say that Brodeur was more than a great regular-season goalie. He got even better when more was on the line. In the playoffs, Brodeur had a record 24 shutouts. One of Brodeur's shutouts came when the stakes were the highest. In the 2003 Stanley Cup Final, Brodeur's New Jersey Devils faced the Anaheim Mighty Ducks. He earned 3 shutouts in the series, including a Game 7 shutout. That shutout clinched the championship for the Devils.

Many hockey records have stood the test of time. Many athletes have tried to break them. Some have come close. Some believe these records are unbreakable. Only time will tell.

Brodeur stands with his goalie mask lifted as the teams' starting lineups are announced before the hockey game begins.

CHAPTER FIVE

Marc-André Fleury

Chasing Brodeur's Record

Marc-André Fleury, a celebrated Canadian hockey goaltender, is known for his agility, reflexes, and athleticism. Fleury was drafted first overall by the Pittsburgh Penguins in 2003. He played a critical role in their Stanley Cup victories in 2009, 2016, and 2017. After moving to the Vegas Golden Knights in 2017, Fleury helped that team reach the Stanley Cup Final in its first season. Known as "Flower" by fans and teammates, Fleury currently plays for the Minnesota Wild. He is twelfth on the list of career shutouts with 75 as of November 2024.

Think FAST!

Test your new knowledge of hockey by answering the following questions.

1. **What are the five different ways a hockey player can score a goal?**

2. **What was Joe Malone's nickname?**

3. **What is written on the Stanley Cup?**

4. **Why did coaches think Henri Richard might not be able to play in the NHL?**

5. **How many goals did Mike Bossy score in his rookie season?**

6. **Why did Mike Bossy retire early?**

7. **How many NHL records does Wayne Gretzky hold?**

8. **What active NHL player is close to passing Gretzky's all-time goals record?**

9. **How fast can an NHL player shoot the puck?**

10. **What is the trophy for the best goaltender? Who is it named after?**

Answers: 1. Full strength, short-handed, power-play, penalty shot, empty net 2. Phantom 3. Names of the players from the winning team 4. They thought he was too small. 5. 53 6. He had a chronic back injury. 7. 61 8. Alex Ovechkin 9. More than 100 miles (161 km) per hour 10. Vezina Trophy. It is named after goalie George Vezina who played for the Montreal Canadiens.

Glossary

agility
The ability to move quickly and easily

anticipate
Expect or predict

chronic
Occurring repeatedly over time

free agency
A state in which a player can sign a contract with any team

impact
A strong effect on someone or something

inscribed
Written on metal, wood, or stone

power-play goal
A goal scored against a team with a player in the penalty box

prolific
Achieving high numbers

rookie
A first-year player

sniper
A hockey player who shoots swiftly and accurately from unexpected positions

tuberculosis
An infectious disease that affects the lungs

Find Out More

IN PRINT

Anderson, Josh. *G.O.A.T. Hockey Goalies*. Lerner Publications, 2024.

Berglund, Bruce. *Hockey GOATs : The Greatest Athletes of All Time*. Capstone Press, 2024.

Donnelly, Patrick. *Football Records That Will Be Tough to Beat*. Mitchell Lane Publishers, 2026.

ON THE INTERNET

***ESPN*, n.d.**
www.espn.com.

***National Hockey League (NHL)*, n.d.**
www.nhl.com.

***Sports Illustrated*, n.d.**
www.si.com.

Index

About the Author

Carla Mooney is the author of many books for young adults and children. She lives in Pittsburgh, Pennsylvania, with her husband and three children. She is an avid hockey fan and goalie mom.